What We Do in Advent

An Anglican Kids' Activity Book

Anne E. Kitch

Illustrations by Dorothy Thompson Perez

MOREHOUSE PUBLISHING

Morehouse Publishing, P.O. Box 1321, Harrisburg, PA 17105

Morehouse Publishing, 445 Fifth Avenue, New York, NY 10016

Morehouse Publishing is an imprint of Church Publishing Incorporated.

Cover image by Dorothy Thompson Perez

Cover design by Jennifer Glosser

Interior design by Beth Oberholtzer

Library of Congress Cataloging-in-Publication Data

Kitch, Anne E.
  What we do in Advent : an Anglican kids' activity book / Anne E. Kitch ; illustrations by Dorothy Thompson Perez.
    p. cm.
  Includes bibliographical references.
  ISBN-13: 978-0-8192-2195-7 (pbk.)
  1. Advent—Juvenile literature. 2. Christmas—Juvenile literature. 3. Christian education of children. 4. Christian education—Activity programs. I. Perez, Dorothy Thompson. II. Title.
  BV40.K58 2006
  263'.912—dc22
                                        2006008881

Printed in the United States of America

06 07 08 09   10 9 8 7 6 5 4 3 2 1

Keeping the Holidays Holy

More and more our commercial culture imposes its timing and taste onto our holidays. This is perhaps most evident in the month before Christmas when we are surrounded by symbols that have nothing to do with the birth of Christ. It is important for those of us in Christian households to reclaim the holidays. In fact, the word "holiday" comes from the practice of keeping "Holy Days." We need to remind ourselves and our children that Christmas comes from Christ's Mass, a feast dedicated to the coming of the Christ, and that Santa Claus is really St. Nicholas, a fourth-century bishop. One way to prepare for a holy Christmas is to honor the season of Advent.

Advent marks the start of the Church year and begins four Sundays before Christmas. It is a time of waiting, and, like any beginning, it holds expectation and promise. During the Advent season we wait for the coming of the Messiah, who we know as Jesus Christ. On the one hand this means waiting for the birth of a child in the manger at Bethlehem; yet Advent is also the time that we wait expectantly for the second coming, the appearance of Christ our King and the completion of God's creation, the fullness of the Kingdom of God.

We cannot prevent ourselves or our children from being bombarded by cultural messages telling us how to celebrate the holidays and what to buy to make them special. But we can speak our values just as clearly. In this book, you'll find enjoyable activities that will enrich your children's experience of Advent as well as teach them more about the traditional events in which they will participate. Prepare for Christmas with an Advent Wreath in your home; celebrate the Feast of St. Nicholas on December 6; say a blessing over your Christmas Tree; say a family prayer around the crèche; celebrate all twelve days of Christmas, up to the Feast of the Epiphany on January 6.

We can choose where our children learn about celebration and keeping holy days: at the mall, on television, from their friends—or in the bosom of their families.

How to Use this Book

This activity book follows the Advent and Christmas season from the first Sunday of Advent through the Feast of the Epiphany on January 6. It includes activities that explore the themes of Advent, Christmas, and Epiphany and mark the saints' days that fall during this part of the Church year.

The activities in this book are best utilized one page at a time, rather than coloring it all at once. Also, the more an adult interacts with the child when using this material, the more engaging the experience will be.

Families

This book can be used at home by families as adults and children learn together about Advent. While the pages can be used in any order, they are organized chronologically and can be used one a day as a counting book toward Christmas and Epiphany.

Christian Educators

Christian educators will find this book useful in a parish setting for Church School classes and children's worship times. The pages can easily be used to supplement Sunday Kid's Packs. The activities will help children better understand and recognize the beginning of the Church Year and the themes of Advent, Christmas, and Epiphany, as well as the biblical story of the coming of Christ.

Using this book with non-readers

Toddlers and preschool children respond to the world around them with their senses. They are aware of what they see, hear, touch, and smell even before they have words to describe these things. They can happily engage with the pages on their own with some crayons or markers. Then they can engage at a deeper level when an adult sits down and reads the pages to them.

Using this book with readers

Early elementary children will enjoy reading the pages on their own. However, don't miss the opportunity of learning from them by engaging in conversation about waiting and the expectations of Advent.

The First Sunday of Advent

Draw the advent candles and light the first candle.
Color 3 candles purple and 1 candle pink.

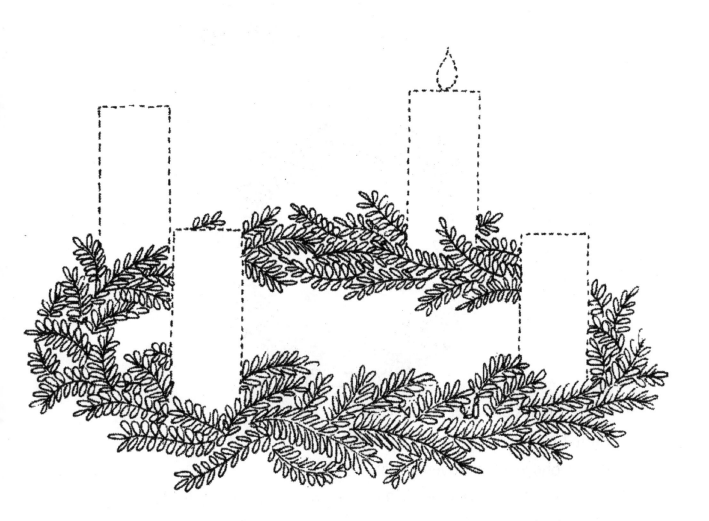

And what I say to you I say to all: Keep awake. (Mark 13:37)

The Advent Wreath

To make your own Advent wreath you will need:

4 candles

4 candle holders

some greens

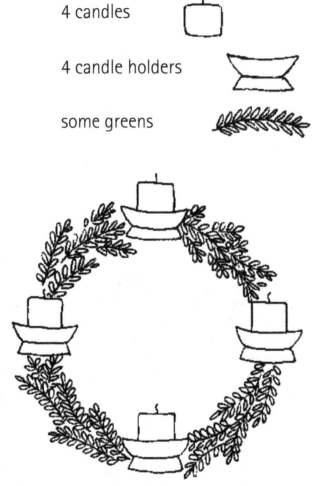

- Place candles and greens in a circle.
- Light 1 candle during the first week of Advent, 2 candles during the second week of advent, and so on.
- Candles can be any color, but 3 purple and 1 rose are traditional. The rose candle is lit on the third Sunday of Advent.

Candles – Light of Christ; Greens – life; Circle - eternity

The Season of Advent

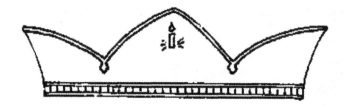

The word Advent means _____. During

the Season of Advent we _____ for the

coming of Christ. We look forward to the

_____ of the baby Jesus. We also expect the

return of Christ our _____.

the coming   birth   King   prepare

Colors of Advent

During Advent, we use the color _____ in church. Advent is a time of waiting for the birth of Jesus and for the return of Christ the King.

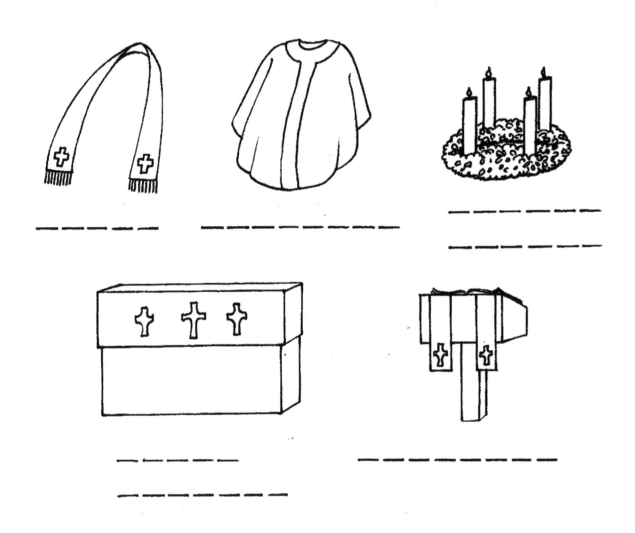

Write the names under the objects and color them the Advent color used in your church.

advent wreath   stole   hangings

chasuble   altar frontal

Church Year Calendar

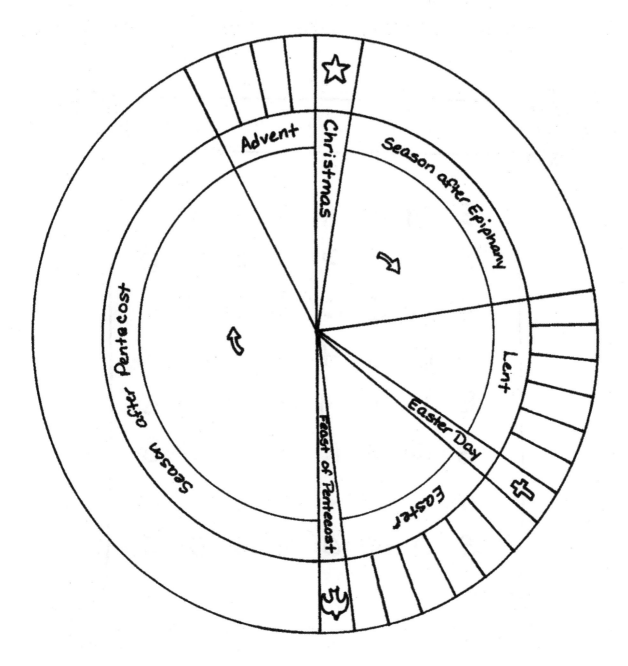

Advent is the beginning of the Church Year. Each Church season has a different color. Color the seasons according to the key:

Green – Season after Pentecost and Epiphany

Blue (or Purple) - Advent

Gold – Christmas and Easter

Red – Pentecost

Purple – Lent

Names of Jesus

We call Jesus by many names. Find and circle these names of Jesus.

E M M A N U E L L
S H E P H E R D
A B S C R D E F
J G S H A I J K
E L I M B N O L
S Q A R B S T O
U C H R I S T R
S O N O F G O D

Christt   Emmanuel   Jesus

Lord   Messiah   Rabbi

Shepherd   Son of God

And you will name him Jesus. (Luke 1:31)

The Feast of St. Nicholas
December 6th

St. Nicholas was the Bishop of Myra. He is the patron saint of children and sailors and is often shown holding three golden balls . to represent his generosity. He loved God and lived a life serving others until his death in 343 CE.

Connect the dots on St. Nicholas' head to draw his Mitre. Draw a gift in his open hand.

The Second Sunday in Advent

Color the blocks according to the key to find the straight path to meet Jesus.

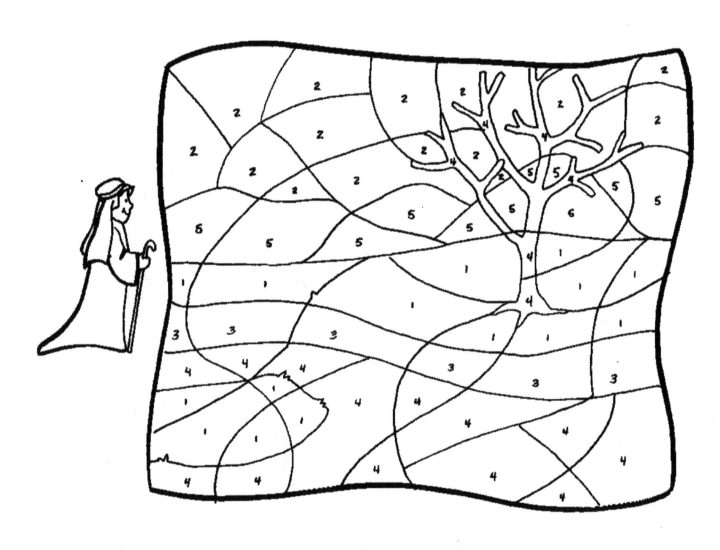

1 = green   2 = blue   3 = yellow
4 = brown   5 = purple

Prepare the way of the Lord, make his paths straight. Mark 1:3

Prophets

A prophet carries God's promises to the people and shows God's love by living and telling God's story. Follow the paths to see what each prophet said about Jesus.

Isaiah 4:6   **Jeremiah 33:15**   **Micah 5:5**

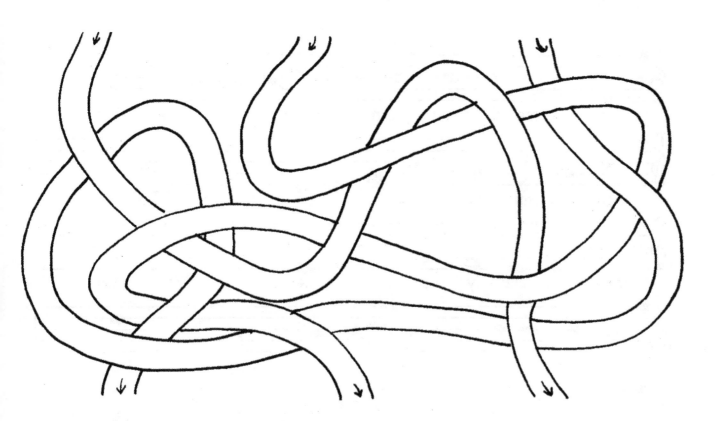

"From Bethlehem will come one to rule Israel."   "A righteous branch will spring up from the house of David."   "He will be called the Prince of Peace."

Advent Carol

Emmanuel means "God with us." Prepare for Advent by singing this carol.

Advent Word Search

Find these Advent words:

LIGHT　　　　　CHRIST　　　　　BIRTH

BETHLEHEM　　　WAITING　　　　KING

GOD

B E T H L E H E M
I C H R I S T K A
R A B E G O D I C
T O K E H R E N H
H W A I T I N G L

"The light shines in the darkness, and the darkness did not overcome it."
(John 1:5)

The Annunciation

In the sixth month the Angel _____ was sent by God to a town in Galilee called Nazareth, to a virgin engaged to a man whose name was _____, of the house of David. The virgin's name was _____. And he came to her and said, "Greetings favored one! The Lord is with you." But she was much perplexed by his words and pondered what sort of greeting this might be. The Angel said to her, "Do not be afraid, Mary, for you have found favor with God. And now you will conceive in your womb and bear a son, and you will name him _____." Luke 1:26-31

Mary   **Jesus**   **Gabriel**   **Joseph**

Color Mary's home town of Nazareth.

Gabriel Visits Mary

Draw the Angel Gabriel telling Mary about her special baby.

Joseph's Dream

Use the underlined words to fill out the crossword puzzle.

An <u>angel</u> of the Lord appeared to him in a <u>dream</u> and said, "<u>Joseph</u>, son of David, do not be afraid to take <u>Mary</u> as your wife, for the <u>child</u> conceived in her is from the <u>Holy Spirit</u>." Matthew 1:20

The Feast of St. Lucy
December 13th

Draw 4 flames on the candles in St. Lucy's crown. Draw a food offering on the plate she is holding. Color the picture (color the sash red).

St. Lucy was a young girl who loved God. The name Lucy means, "light." She is the patron saint of eyesight. In Sweden, her feast is celebrated by a young girl wearing a crown of candles as she offers food to her family. Her sash is red because St. Lucy was a martyr, someone who died for her faith.

The Third Sunday in Advent

The Messiah who is coming is mighty.

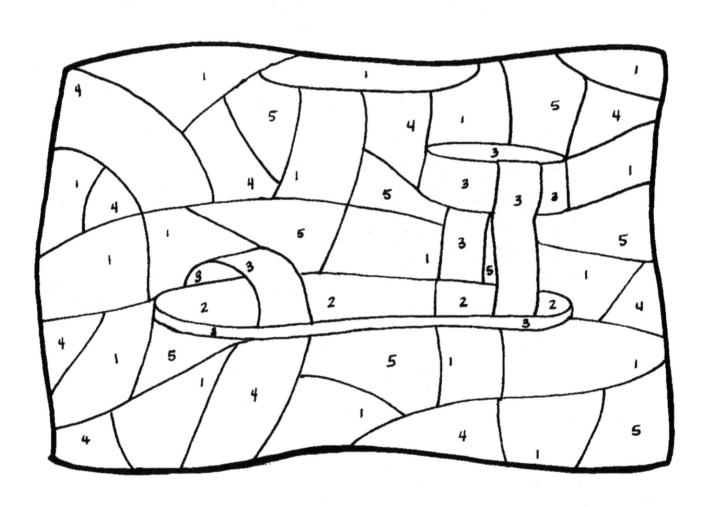

Color the picture according to the key to discover the hidden picture:

1 – Purple

2 – Yellow

3 – Brown

4 – Blue

5 – Green

John the Baptist said, "I am not worthy to untie the thong of his sandals."
Luke 3:16

The Peaceable Kingdom

Connect the dots and color the picture.

"The wolf shall live with the lamb, the leopard shall lie down with the kid, the calf and the lion and fatling together, and a little child shall lead them." Isaiah 11:6

The Visitation

In those days Mary set out and went with haste to a Judean town in the hill country, where she entered the house of Zechariah and greeted Elizabeth. When _____ heard Mary's greeting, the _____ leaped in her womb. And Elizabeth was filled with the _____ and exclaimed in a loud cry, "Blessed are you among women and blessed is the fruit of your womb." And Mary said, "My soul magnifies the Lord and my Spirit rejoices in _____ my Savior." Luke 1:39-42, 46-47

Elizabeth   **Holy Spirit**   **Child**   **God**

Help Mary find her way to Elizabeth's house.

Mary Visits her Cousin Elizabeth

1 – Red

2 – Blue

4 – Brown

5 – Purple

3 – Yellow

Color by number.

Building the City of Bethlehem

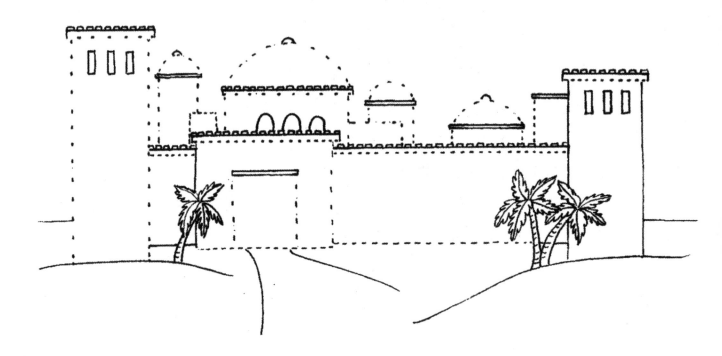

Trace the dotted lines to finish building the city of Bethlehem. Add some more homes.

Getting Ready for Christmas

Connect the dots to find a Christmas symbol that
represents everlasting life.

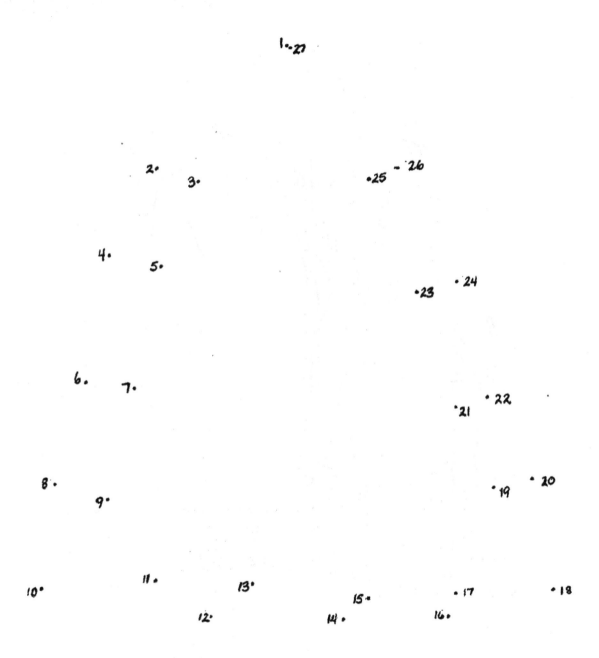

People used to bring evergreens inside during the winter to remind them
that there is always new life and that spring would come again. As
Christians we use this symbol to remind us that Jesus is the new life that
God has sent us. Decorate your picture to celebrate the birth of Christ.

The Fourth Sunday of Advent

In those days a decree went out from Emperor Augustus that all the world should be registered. All went to their own towns to be registered. Joseph also went from the town of Nazareth in Galilee to Judea, to the city of David called Bethlehem, because he was descended from the house and family of David. He went to be registered with Mary, to whom he was engaged and who was expecting a child. Luke 2:1, 3-5

Journey to Bethlehem

Trace a path for Mary and Joseph to follow from Nazareth to Bethlehem.

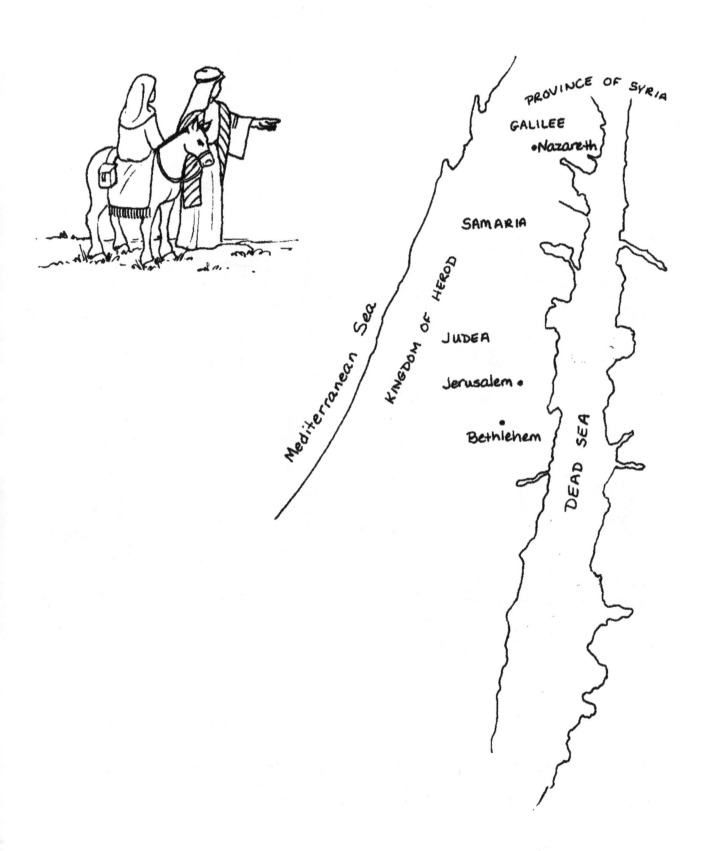

No Room at the Inn

When Mary and Joseph arrived at Bethlehem, the city was full of visitors.
They could not find any room left at the inn.

There are seven things that are different between these inn doors.
Circle the differences you can find.

Animals at the Stable

Count the animals that live at the stable.

How many . . .

How many animals
altogether?

The Feast of St. Thomas
December 21st

Help St. Thomas carry the Good News to the church.

St. Thomas was a disciple of Jesus who also became an apostle. After the death and resurrection of Jesus, St. Thomas carried the good news to many places. Tradition says he traveled as far as India.

The Shepherds

In that region there were shepherds living in the fields, keeping watch over their flock by night. Then an angel of the Lord stood before them and the glory of the Lord shone around them, and they were terrified. But the angel said to them, "Do not be afraid; for see — I am bringing you good news of great joy for all the people: to you is born this day in the city of David a Savior, who is the Messiah, the Lord." Luke 2:8-11

How many?

____ 🧑‍🦯

____ ✳

____ 🐑

____ ✴

The Heavenly Host

Suddenly there was with the angel a multitude of the heavenly host praising God and saying, "Glory to God in the highest heaven, and on earth peace among those who he favors." Luke 2:13-14

Find 12 angels of the heavenly host surrounding the angel Gabriel in the stained glass window. Color the picture.

Silent Night

Si - lent night, ho - ly night, all is calm,

all is bright round yon Vir - gin mother and child

Ho - ly Infant so ten - der and mild, sleep in heavenly

peace. Sleep in hea - ven - ly peace.

Christmas Eve

"And she gave birth to her first born son and wrapped him in bands of cloth, and laid him in a manger, because there was no place for them in the inn." Luke 2:7

Draw the baby Jesus in the manger.

Christmas Gift

Jesus is the special gift that God gives us at Christmas. Draw a picture of a special gift you would like to give.

Who would you like to give this gift to?

Looking for Christmas

With the Light of Christ I can see three presents and a Christmas tree.
A wreath, two candles shining bright and St. Nicholas almost out of sight.

Find and color the hidden pictures.

Looking for Jesus

With the Light of Christ I can see two angels singing joyfully, three shepherds watching from afar, the baby Jesus and a star.

Find the hidden pictures and color the scene.

Prepare the House

Decorate this house for Christmas.

The Feast of St. Stephen
December 26th

St. Stephen was one of the first people chosen by the Apostles to be a deacon, a person whose ministry is taking care of people's everyday needs. He is shown wearing a deacon's stole over his left shoulder, holding an alms box to collect money for the poor, and carrying incense for worship.

Color the picture of St. Stephen.

The Feast of St. John
December 27th

St. John was a disciple of Jesus and is known as an evangelist because he wrote one of the four gospels. He is shown holding a chalice, or large cup. A story is told how he was given a cup of poisoned wine, but when he blessed it the wine became pure.

Color each piece of the stained glass window with these colors:

1 – Pink	3 – Red	5 – Brown
2 – Blue	4 – Yellow	

The Feast of the Epiphany
January 6th

Help the Magi Follow the star to find Jesus.

After Jesus was born in Bethlehem of Judea, wise men from the East came to Jerusalem, asking, "Where is the child who has been born king of the Jews? For we observed his star at its rising and have come to pay him homage." Matthew 2:1-2

Adoration of the Magi

On entering the house, they saw the child with Mary his mother; and they knelt down and paid him homage. Then, opening their treasure chests, they offered him gifts of gold, frankincense and myrrh. Matthew 2:11-12

Trace the gifts that the Magi are offering Jesus. Draw Jesus receiving the gifts.

December Saint Feast Days

Complete the crossword puzzle to find the saints honored during the season of Advent with a symbol that represents them.

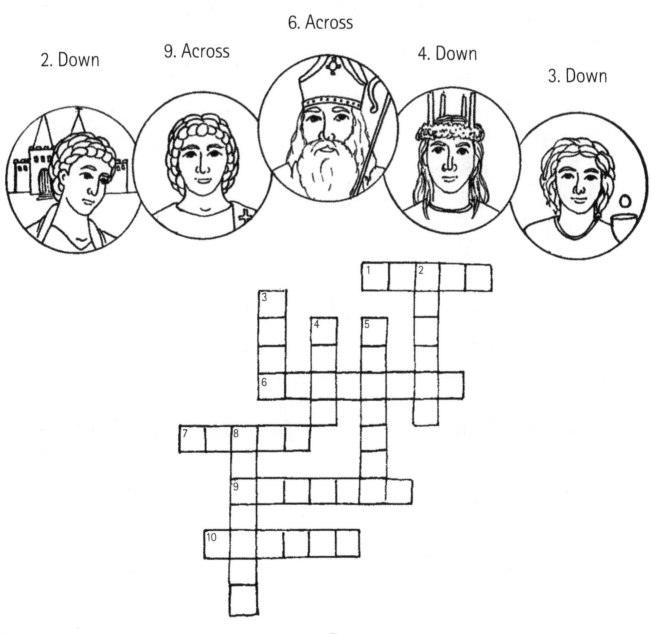

2. Down   9. Across   6. Across   4. Down   3. Down

Across:
1. St. Nicholas wore a _____.
7. Lucy means _____.
10. St. Stephan was the first_____.

Down:
5. St. Thomas was an _____.
8. John wrote one of the _____.

Answers

Names of Jesus

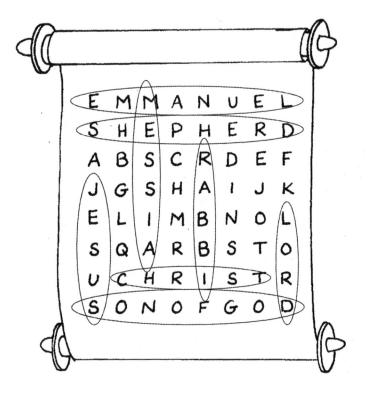

Advent Word Search

No Room at the Inn

1. Door knocker
2. Lantern on left
3. Door number on right
4. Handles
5. Door matte
6. Peep holes
7. Hinges

December Saint Feast Days

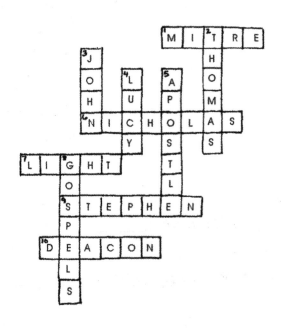

The Church Year

The Church year consists of two great feasts: Easter Day, the date of which is movable, and Christmas Day, which is always December 25. (Easter Day is always the first Sunday after the full moon that falls on or after March 21.) Based on these two feasts, the Church Year is divided into seasons: Advent, Christmas, Epiphany, Lent, Easter, and Pentecost.

Advent, which means "the coming," is the beginning of the Church year and begins four Sundays before Christmas. During Advent we wait for the birth of Christ and we anticipate Christ's second coming. The color for Advent is usually purple (for royalty) or blue (for peace).

We celebrate Christmas, or the Feast of the Nativity, for twelve days, from December 25 to January 6. The color for Christmas is white or gold (for purity and new life). January 6 is the feast of the Epiphany, when we celebrate the visit of the Magi to the Christ child. The color for the Feast of Epiphany is white, but the Sundays following Epiphany are green (for growth, hope, and revelation). The Epiphany season runs from January 6 to Ash Wednesday and varies in length from six to nine weeks.

Ash Wednesday is the beginning of Lent. Lent is the forty days before Easter and is a time of fasting and preparation for the great celebration of Easter. The forty days represent the time Jesus spent fasting in the wilderness at the beginning of his ministry. The five Sundays in Lent are not considered fast days and are not counted in the forty. The color for lent is usually purple (royalty and penitence), but some churches use vestments in a Lenten array, rough or homespun fabric with no color (for simplicity). Lent ends with Holy Week: Palm Sunday, Maundy Thursday, Good Friday, and Holy Saturday. The color for

Holy Week is red (which is the color of blood).

The Easter Season begins with the Great Vigil of Easter on Easter Eve followed by Easter Day, or the Sunday of the Resurrection. We celebrate Easter for fifty days, called The Great Fifty Days, until the Feast of Pentecost. On the fortieth day of Easter we celebrate Ascension Day, the day that the resurrected Christ ascended into Heaven. The color of Easter is white or gold (again purity and new life).

On the Feast of Pentecost, the last day of the Easter Season, we celebrate the coming of the Holy Spirit and the beginning of the Church. The color for the Feast of Pentecost is red (for fire and the Holy Spirit). The time after Pentecost until Advent is called the Season after Pentecost. The color for this season is green (for growth and hope).

The Power of Symbols

In Anglican tradition, we understand the power of ritual and symbol. Most churches are full of symbols that engage us in worship and teach us about God. These trappings change from season to season and Advent is full of them.

Sometime during the Advent season, take a walk with a child through your church. What do you see, hear, smell? Are there stained glass windows? What stories do they tell? Is there an Advent wreath? How many candles are lit? Are there greens hanging in the church? Are there Christian symbols on kneelers, or altar hangings? What do they represent? Are there memorials that tell stories about the parish and its people? All of these things testify to the Glory of God and enhance the richness of our worship.

Saints of the Church

Saints are men and women of the past whom the Church honors for their witness to Christ. They are people recognized by those around them to have had an extraordinary commitment to Christ and to have exhibited steadfast faith sometimes even at the cost of their lives. They are not by any means perfect, but rather they lived lives in which the presence of Christ shone forth by their words and actions. Some of the attributes of saints include heroic faith, love, goodness of life, joyousness, service to others for Christ's sake, and devotion. Each saint that the church recognizes is assigned a specific date for commemoration, called a feast day. For a list of saints recognized by the Episcopal Church, their feast dates, and their stories, see *Lesser Feasts and Fasts 2003* (Church Publishing).

Advent and Christmas Rituals for the Home

For prayers to use with your advent wreath and blessings for your Christmas Tree and crèche, see *The Anglican Family Prayer Book*.

Glossary

Advent: The first season of the Church year. It is the four weeks before Christmas.

Advent Wreath: A circle of greens with four candles which are usually purple. Sometimes a white candle, the Christ Candle, is placed in the center. The purple candles are lit one by one on the four Sundays before Christmas. The Christ candle is lit on Christmas Eve.

Alms box: A box, usually with a slot in the lid, used to collect money offerings to be used for those in need.

Altar frontal: A decorative cloth than hangs over the front of the altar often decorated with Christian symbols. Its color usually matches the color of the Church Season.

Angel: A being that acts as God's messenger. The Greek word *angelos* means to announce. From it we also get the word "evangelism," to bear a message.

The Annunciation of our Lord: The feast day on which we remember the Angel Gabriel announcing to Mary that she will be the mother of Jesus, God's son. We celebrate this feast on March 25.

Apostle: A person who carries a specific message to someone. In the early church, the followers of Jesus who went out to carry the good news of Christ and to teach his message were called the Apostles. Some, but not all, of the disciples became apostles.

Bethlehem: A small village in the southern part of the Holy Land

Chalice: A large cup, often made of silver (but can be pottery or glass), used for the wine during communion.

Chasuble: A large oval garment without sleeves that a priest wears when celebrating the Eucharist. Its color often matches the color of the Church season.

Christ: The word "Christ" means anointed one. Jesus is the Christ, God's anointed one who came to save the world.

Deacon: An ordained minister whose call is to serve the people and who assists bishops and priest during worship.

Disciple: A follower of Jesus. Jesus had twelve disciples that were close to him and had special duties, but there were many more disciples who traveled with him throughout the Holy Land and learned from him.

Emmanuel (also Immanuel): A name that means "God is with us." The prophets used this name to refer to the messiah who was to come.

Epiphany: The feast day on which we remember the visit of the magi to the Christ Child. The Feast of the Epiphany is celebrated on January 6. The Season after Epiphany lasts until Ash Wednesday, from six to nine weeks.

Evangelist: A person who tells the good news. The saints Matthew, Mark, Luke, and John are called the four Evangelists because they each wrote a gospel about the life of Jesus.

Galilee: A region in the northern part of the Holy Land along the Sea of Galilee. The village of Nazareth is in Galilee.

Gospel: One of the four first-hand accounts of the life and teaching of Jesus contained in the New Testament (Matthew, Mark, Luke, and John). During the Eucharist, the Gospel is read by one of the clergy, preferably a deacon. The word "gospel" means "good news."

Hangings: Decorated bands of cloth hung from the lectern or pulpit that match the liturgical color of the season.

Icon: A flat picture of a sacred person, usually painted on wood but sometimes made of mosaic or other materials. Icons have a specific tradition to their style and production. Each icon is "written" by an individual iconographer.

Incense: a resin that produces fragrant smoke when burned. It is traditionally used for worship as a symbol of our prayers rising to God. Often a deacon will cense the gospel book before reading the gospel during the Eucharist.

Judea: A region in the southern part of the Holy Land which included the cities of Jerusalem and Bethlehem.

Magi: The wise sages who came to visit the Christ child in Bethlehem. Also known as the wise men. The word "magi" comes from the Greek word *magoi* which is used in the New Testament (Matthew 2:1).

Martyr: A person who suffers death for refusing to renounce their faith.

Messiah: The expected king and deliverer of the people of God. Jesus was the messiah.

Mitre: A large hat worn by a bishop as a sign of office.

Nazareth: A small village in the north of the Holy Land.

Pentecost: The feast day on which we celebrate the coming of the Holy Spirit. Pentecost is the Sunday that falls fifty days after Easter Sunday.

Prophet: A person who is called by God to speak and act on God's message for the people. Prophets warn people about problems and tell of blessings to come. The prophets who spoke about the coming of the Messiah include Isaiah, Micah, and Jeremiah.

Rabbi: A wise Jewish teacher. Jesus was called Rabbi by his disciples.

Stole: A band of cloth, usually the color of the liturgical season or occasion, worn by a priest or bishop over both shoulders as a sign of office. A deacon wears a stole over the left shoulder.

The Visitation of the Blessed Virgin Mary: The feast day on which we remember Mary's visit to her cousin Elizabeth after the Annunciation. Elizabeth recognizes that Mary is pregnant with the Christ child (Luke 1:39–56). The feast of the Visitation is celebrated on May 31.

References

Guilbert, Charles Mortimer. *Words of Our Worship*. New York: Church Publishing, 1988.

Kitch, Anne E. *The Anglican Family Prayer Book*. Harrisburg, Pa.: Morehouse Publishing, 2004.

Lesser Feasts and Fasts 2003. New York: Church Publishing, 2003.

CPSIA information can be obtained
at www.ICGtesting.com
Printed in the USA
JSHW060919050822
28933JS00001B/1